CRITICAL ACCLAIM FOR JAM
THE BATTLE CRY O.
Pulitzer Prize Winner

"This is magic.... I was swept away, feeling as if I had never heard the saga before.... Accounts of the Civil War usually sacrifice either detail to narrative flow, or narrative to detail. Mr. McPherson does neither.... This is historical writing of the highest order."
The New York Times Book Review

"Absolutely brilliant.... The finest single volume on the war and its background. *Battle Cry of Freedom* is a beautifully written narrative."
The Washington Post Book World

"Splendid.... Looks like the standard for the next three decades."
Newsweek

"A vivid portrait of antebellum America.... McPherson seems to have picked out the richest of the copiously rich Civil War material.... It must surely be, of the 50,000 books written on the Civil War, the finest compression of that national paroxysm ever fitted between two covers."
Los Angeles Times

"Brisk, lively, even at times tart.... Grant, Lee, Sherman, Jeb Stuart, Stonewall Jackson, so many others: an American military pantheon. McPherson does his starry cast justice. He brings to vivid life not just commanding officers, but enlisted men, politicians, Abolitionists, Southern fire-eaters, Northern barn-burners, Copperheads, Know-Nothings."
The Boston Sunday Globe

"McPherson handles all ... with a beautifully organized, compelling narrative and prose whose occasional leap into modern ebullience should captivate a new generation of Civil War readers."
Chicago Tribune

"This is an epic story told in epic style, written in clear, luminous prose.... A zesty, meaty intellectual feast that will nourish and satisfy the reader."
The Houston Post

"Exhaustively researched, written with skill and assurance.... This book may not be superseded in our time."
Newsday

James M. McPherson
Is Blood Thicker Than Water?

James M. McPherson is best known for his classic work on the American Civil War, *The Battle Cry of Freedom*, which won the Pulitzer Prize for non-fiction. He is also the author of many other books on the subject, including *Ordeal By Fire*, *The Atlas of The Civil War*, *Marching Toward Freedom* and *The Abolitionist Legacy*. He is a professor in the Department of History at Princeton University.

Is Blood Thicker Than Water?

IS BLOOD THICKER
THAN WATER?

Crises of Nationalism
in the Modern World

JAMES M. MCPHERSON

Vintage Canada
A Division of Random House of Canada

Canadian Cataloguing in Publication Data

McPherson, James M.

Is blood thicker than water?:
crises of nationalism in the modern world

(The Barbara Frum lecture series)

ISBN: 0-679-30928-4

1. Nationalism.   I. Title.   II. Series.

JC311.M239 1998   320.54   C97-932292-8

Printed and bound in the United States

10   9   8   7   6   5   4   3   2   1

For Jenny and Jeff

TABLE OF CONTENTS

Acknowledgments

I am grateful to David Frum and his family for the opportunity to deliver the Barbara Frum Lecture in honor of the memory of one of Canada's foremost journalists. I am also indebted to David Frum for his initial suggestion of a topic for this lecture, the origins of civil wars, which set me to thinking about nationalism. To a native Canadian whom I have never met, Michael Ignatieff, I owe an intellectual debt of sizable proportions; his book, *Blood and Belonging: Journeys into the New Nationalism*, provided me with the framework of ethnic and civic nationalism for the lecture and for this book. I must also thank Elisabeth Sifton of Hill and Wang Publishers for calling *Blood and Belonging* to my attention. Doug Pepper of Random House of Canada has been a most encouraging editor who suggested sources to help me overcome my embarrassing ignorance of Canadian history and listened patiently to my half-formed ideas. Professor R. Craig of Toronto University also offered useful suggestions about Canadian sources.

CHAPTER ONE:
A TALE OF TWO NATIONS

THIS IS THE STORY of a geographically large country in North America with a federal form of government. The population of this country considered themselves to be two distinct peoples, each concentrated mostly in a discrete region, with conflicting interests that threatened to divide them into separate nations. What held them together in the early years was a shared fear of domination by another country. As the decades passed, the people in one region remained mostly rural and agricultural, conservative in their cultural and religious outlook, with minimal educational facilities that served the elite but left many of the rest illiterate. The other region diversified its economy, established a flourishing system of education that created almost universal literacy, built an impressive transportation infrastructure, experienced growing urbanization, and attracted most of the large number of immigrants who entered the country to gain the benefits of its dynamic economy. As a consequence, this region grew in population, prosperity, and cultural diversity faster than the other region, which saw its share of the national population gradually shrink from half to little more than a quarter.

These developments kindled the smouldering tensions that had always existed between the two peoples. Bankers, investors, and industrialists in the more modernized region gained control of sectors of the other's economy. Cultural leaders in the more advanced region disparaged the backwardness of those in the other. The increasingly multicultural society of the majority population, which had expanded into a continent-wide affiliation of like-minded regions, provoked a fierce defensive response in the other, which closed ranks in an aggressive reaffirmation of its distinct society. A not-so-quiet revolution of cultural and economic nationalism emerged in the minority region to modernize its economy, improve its educational system, raise the consciousness and self-confidence of its people, and liberate them from a self-perceived colonial subordination to the majority and make them masters in their own house.

Political power became a weapon in the minority's effort to consolidate its distinctiveness in its home region and protect its status in the larger federation. At home a militant regional party enacted restrictive legislation against those suspected of identifying with the majority in the rest of the country. This legislation had the effect of forcing many within the minority region to emigrate — a consequence not unwelcome to those who intended to become masters in their own house.

So long as the minority region remained in the national federation, however, its people continued to fear a threat from without to their distinct society within. To ward off this threat, they turned to coalition politics and a quest for constitutional reform at the federal level. Over a period of several decades, a majority of voters in the minority region combined with fluctuating pluralities of voters in other regions, and they won control of the federal government most of the time for more than half a century. During much of that time, a political leader from the minority region was head of the federal government. As the not-so-quiet revolution of consciousness raising accelerated in the minority region, the federal government under this party leaned over backwards to accommodate many of the demands from the minority region to protect its special interests.

These accommodations did not go far enough for some leaders in the minority region, whose decreasing proportion of the national population created something of a siege mentality. Many residents of this region became convinced that, if they were to remain masters in their own house, they must take that house out of the national federation; the two peoples must become two nations. As a step in that direction — or perhaps as a step to forestall it from happening, depending on one's point of view — a political leader in the minority region proposed a form of sovereignty association in which the minority and majority regions would each exercise a separate sovereignty over most matters of domestic concern within its borders.

This proposal did not win majority support even in the minority region. But the fall-out from divisive debates about it increased the efforts of federal leaders to come up with political and constitutional compromises to assuage the fears and demands of the minority region in order to deter its secession. The main result of these efforts was a further polarization of the country. The proposed compromises did not go far enough to placate the minority section and went much too far for many voters elsewhere. A growing hostility towards recognition of a distinct society in the minority region and the granting of special favours to it fuelled a political backlash in the rest of the country, especially in areas the most distant from the minority region. A new party was born in those distant areas and quickly forged into mainstream status, virtually destroying two other parties. Two last-ditch proposals for constitutional compromises to avert a pending split into two nations went down to defeat. A majority in the rest of the country made it clear that they were willing to risk the secession of the minority region rather than concede to its demands for more powers. The nation seemed on the brink of meltdown.

In 1861, it did melt down. I have been describing the history of the United States from its founding to the secession of Southern States in 1860–61. Any resemblance to the history of Canada is more than coincidental. There are striking parallels in the experiences of these two North American nations, though one must be careful not to push the analogy too far. The chief difference, of course, lies in the causes of Québécois and Southern separatism: language and culture in one case; slavery in the other. And, while the United States was formed of a voluntary union between Free and Slave States, the forerunner of Canada was formed of the conquest of one people by another. Nevertheless, the British North America Act creating the Dominion of Canada in 1867 gave birth to a tradition of two coequal founding peoples united voluntarily in a federal union.

Despite obvious differences, the similarities between the United States after 1787 and Canada after 1837 are instructive. At the constitutional convention in 1787, delegate Pierce Butler of South Carolina remarked that the two peoples of the Southern and Northern States had conflicting interests that were "as different as the interests of Russia and Turkey."[1] Seventy years later, the Charleston *Mercury*, a leading Southern Rights newspaper, reiterated that, "on the subject of slavery, the South and the North ... are not only two Peoples, but they are rival, hostile Peoples." On the other side of the Mason–Dixon line, the antislavery New York

Tribune agreed that "we are not one people. We are two peoples. We are a people for Freedom and a people for Slavery. Between the two, conflict is inevitable."[2]

Similarly, after the uprising of French Canadians against British rule in Lower Canada in 1837, the Earl of Durham, sent to govern Canada, wrote in his famous report of 1839 that "I expected to find a contest between a government and a people. I found two nations warring in the bosom of a single state." More than a century later, a scholar of literature and politics in Quebec wrote that "hating the English has been, since 1840, the motor of French Canadian nationalism."[3]

One of the forces that brought and held the two peoples together in each of these federal unions during the early decades of their histories was the fear of an outside threat — from Britain, in the case of the United States, and from the United States, in the case of Canada. As these fears subsided, centrifugal forces that drove the two peoples apart grew more powerful.

In the United States, the North and South were more alike in 1790 than ever again before the Civil War. Slavery even existed in several Northern States, for the gradual-emancipation laws had not yet fully taken hold. The numbers of people living in "Free" and Slave States were virtually equal. So were their percentages of rural and urban populations. But by 1860 the population of the Free States was 58 per cent greater than that of the Slave States. The number of *free* people in the North was nearly two and one-half times the number in the South, and the urban percentage in the Free States was more than two and one-half times that in the Slave States. During those decades, the Northern economy developed diversified agricultural, commercial, and industrial sectors, while the Southern economy remained overwhelmingly agricultural, and its infrastructure of roads, canals, railroads, and bridges lagged far behind that of the North. In 1810, the Slave States had 31 per cent of the capital invested in manufacturing in the United States; by 1860, this figure had declined to 16 per cent. In 1800, 82 per cent of the Southern labour force worked in agriculture, compared with 68 per cent in the Free States. By 1860, the proportion of the Northern labour force in agriculture had dropped to 40 per cent, while in the South it had actually increased slightly, to 84 per cent. Largely because of these differences, seven-eighths of the immigrants settled in the Free States and twice as many Southern whites migrated to the North as vice versa.[4]

Just as the population of the Free States grew 57 per cent more than that of the Slave States from 1830 to 1860, so the population of Canada outside Quebec grew at a rate 83 per cent greater than that of Quebec from 1961 to 1991. Nearly twice as many people migrated from Quebec to other provinces than migrated into Quebec from the rest of Canada, a ratio similar to intersectional patterns of migration between Slave and Free States in the ante-bellum United States. In 1860, the percentage of the population that was foreign-born was four times greater in the North than the South; in Canada the percentage of immigrants in the population outside Quebec was more than twice the percentage in Quebec in 1991. And despite the growth and diversification of Quebec's economy beginning with the Quiet Revolution of the 1960s, the economic output of the rest of Canada grew at a rate 81 per cent greater than that of Quebec from 1961 to 1991 — a disparity similar to that between the Free and Slave States from 1830 to 1860.[5]

Contrasts between the North and South in the United States stemmed, in part, from their contrasting value systems. "We are an agricultural people," declared one Southern leader proudly in 1861. "We want no manufactures: we desire no trading, no mechanical or manufacturing classes.... As long as we have our rice, our sugar, our tobacco, and our cotton, we can command wealth to purchase all we want." The educated sons of the Southern elite went into the professions or became planters rather than businessmen or bankers. As for the Yankees, said another Southerner, "trade, commerce, the pursuit of gain, manufacture, and the base mechanical arts, had so degraded the whole race" that Southerners could no longer tolerate association with them.[6]

A study of the ante-bellum occupations of Americans distinguished enough to be chronicled in the *Dictionary of American Biography* found that, in proportion to the white population, three times more Northerners than Southerners went into business, and six times as many were engineers or inventors. Similarly, a far smaller percentage of French Canadians than English Canadians before the 1960s became businessmen, inventors, engineers, and the like. "Their educated sons tended to go into the priesthood or the professions," writes one historian of French Canadians. "They had little experience with free-market capitalism and little regard for corporate concentration. Those who had made money in furs or farming were often unwilling to risk it in timber or railways."[7] As a consequence, English Canadians and their capital controlled much of the commercial and industrial economy of Quebec until recent decades. "In Montreal the French outnumber the English three to one," says a bitter young French Canadian in 1918 in Hugh MacLennan's novel *Two Solitudes.* "In the province we outnumber them seven to one. And yet, the English own everything...the big business...the railroads, the banks. What was left to a man like himself but the Church, medicine, or the law?"[8]

A comparable situation prevailed in the antebellum United States. Northern or British firms owned most of the ships that carried Southern cotton to market. Most of the "factors" who extended credit to planters were representatives of Northern banks. "Our whole commerce except a small fraction is in the hands of Northern men," complained a resident of Mobile, Alabama, in 1847. "[Seveneighths] of our bank stock is owned by Northern men.... Our wholesale and retail business — everything in short worth mentioning is in the hands of [Yankees].... Financially we are more enslaved than our negroes." Four years later, an Alabama newspaper lamented that, while "Northerners abuse and denounce slavery and slaveholders, yet our slaves are clothed with Northern manufactured goods, have Northern hats and shoes, work with Northern hoes, ploughs, and other implements.... The slaveholder dresses in Northern goods, rides in a Northern saddle... sports his Northern carriage.... In Northern vessels his products are carried to market, his cotton is ginned with Northern gins, his sugar is crushed and preserved by Northern machinery; his rivers are navigated by Northern steamboats."[9]

Quebec's Quiet Revolution was fuelled, in part, by a desire to overcome a similar colonial economic relationship to English Canada. "An intricate, pervasive drive" to become "masters in our own house," the Quiet Revolution harnessed the forces of "urbanization, industrialization, and secularization" that "transformed Quebec into a modern society that, except for language, was scarcely distinguishable from the rest of North America."[10] Well, not quite. In 1992, the gross domestic product per capita of Ontario was 19 per cent higher than that of Quebec — which, in turn, was also still slightly below the GDP for all of Canada. Nevertheless, Quebeckers did make great strides towards becoming masters in their own house, a process which stoked the fires of Québécois separatism by encouraging confidence that the province could go it alone.

The American South also experienced a quiet revolution of sorts in the 1850s. Its prophet was James B.D. De Bow of New Orleans, who in 1846 founded a magazine with the title *Commercial Review of the South and West*, which soon became known as *De Bow's Review*. Instead of the traditional Southern slogan "Cotton Is King," De Bow put on his masthead the hopeful motto "Commerce Is King." The South could never protect its institutions and rights in the Union, De Bow insisted, or take its place as an independent nation outside the Union, so long as Northerners controlled crucial sectors of the Southern economy. The amount "lost to us annually by our vassalage to the North," wrote De Bow in 1852, was "one hundred million dollars. Great God! Does Ireland sustain a more degrading relation to Great Britain? Will we not throw off this degrading dependence?" De Bow demanded "action! ACTION!! *ACTION!!!* — not in the rhetoric of Congress, but in the busy hum of mechanism, and in the thrifty operations of the hammer and anvil."[11]

De Bow helped organize a series of annual meetings known as the Southern Commercial Conventions to promote this vision. They proposed

Southern-owned shipping lines, railroad construction with Southern capital, textile mills, and other industrial enterprises. "Give us factories, machine shops, work shops," declared a Southern newspaper, and "we shall ere long be able to assert our rights."[12]

Many Southern leaders also deplored the region's educational backwardness and its high rate of illiteracy (20 per cent for whites in 1850). They noted with alarm that some of the best and brightest Southern boys went North to college, and that a shocking number of Southern college presidents, professors, schoolteachers, and even newspaper editors, came from the North. They urged the Southern States to establish and upgrade educational institutions, from the elementary to college level, in order to improve literacy and educate Southerners at home so they could become masters in their own house.

This Southern quiet revolution did accomplish some of its goals in the 1850s. Several Slave States established or expanded public school systems, on paper at least, and several new colleges were founded or chartered. The Slave States more than quadrupled their railroad mileage. Capital invested in Southern manufacturing rose by 77 per cent

(39 per cent per capita) during the decade. The South enjoyed a booming economy and, unlike the North, suffered little from the short but sharp recession of 1857–58.

But this Southern prosperity owed less to industrial development than to a rising world demand for cotton — three-quarters of which was grown in the American South. Cotton, rather than commerce, remained king. "Our cotton is the most wonderful talisman in the world," declared a planter in 1853. "By its power we are transmuting whatever we choose into whatever we want." Like Quebec's exports of hydro-electric power, wood pulp, paper, and other products, the South's exports of cotton gave its leaders confidence that their economy could go it alone. "The slaveholding South is now the controlling power of the world," boasted South Carolina's Senator James Henry Hammond in a famous speech in 1858. "Cotton, rice, tobacco, and naval stores command the world.... No power on earth dares...to make war on cotton. Cotton is king."[13]

This bombast cloaked some fundamental deficiencies and insecurities. The South in 1860 still lagged far behind the North in educational facilities and literacy. And just as Quebec's per-capita income and gross domestic product remained below the national average, and significantly below Ontario's, in 1991, despite the Quiet Revolution, so Southern per-capita income in 1860 was 23 per cent below the national average, and 30 per cent below that of the Free States.[14] Moreover, the South's population, like Quebec's, grew at a slower rate than that of the rest of the country. In Quebec this relative population stagnation caused francophones to feel "insecure and become fearful of their decreasing influence," in the words of a student of Canadian demographic trends. "Insecurity breeds insularity.... This is the fear that motivates many Quebec nationalists toward separation or for more powers in the Constitution."[15]

Similar insecurities beset the American South in the 1850s as the admission of three new Free States to the Union tipped the balance of power in favour of the North for the first time. The future seemed to portend a further decrease in the South's percentage of population and political power within the Union. A desperate sense of beleaguerment, a sort of siege mentality, gripped the Slave States, especially as the rise of the Republican party, with its platform of preventing further expansion of slavery, threatened to encircle the South with Free States and squeeze slavery to death. "Long before the North gets this vast accession of strength," declared James Hammond of South Carolina — the same Hammond who boasted that King Cotton ruled the world — "she will ride over us rough shod, proclaim freedom or something equivalent to it to our Slaves and reduce us to the condition of Hayti [*sic*]. ... If we do not act now, we deliberately consign our children, not our posterity, but our *children* to the flames."[16] When Lincoln's election in 1860 as the first Republican president signified that this frightening future had arrived, the South left the Union.

Before this day of Armageddon, however, the South, like Quebec, had used its political power within the region and its political leverage within the federation to protect its distinctive society. In the South this distinctiveness revolved around the "peculiar institution" of slavery. In Quebec it revolves around the French language and culture. In both cases the perceived collective right of the society to protect its cherished institutions overrode the individual rights of dissenters. The Southern States passed numerous laws prohibiting any expression of antislavery sentiments, banning antislavery publications (this was long before the Supreme Court ruled that the Bill of Rights, including the First

Amendment, applied to the states), made the incitement or encouragement of slave insurrections or escapes capital crimes, and literally put a price on the heads of prominent abolitionists. Critics of slavery had to leave the South and settle in the Free States. Self-appointed vigilantes monitored the movements of Northern businessmen and visitors in the South. In times of tension such as the summer of 1860, those suspected of antislavery sentiments found themselves subject to mob violence and were lucky to escape the region with nothing worse than a coat of tar and feathers.[17]

It may be invidious to compare these repressions to Quebec's Bills 101 and 178 mandating French-language signs and restricting access to English-language schools. The language police, sometimes self-appointed, who roamed English sections of Montreal to enforce the sign laws did not lynch or tar and feather the violators they found. But the defensive–aggressive mentality underlying the language laws in Quebec and gag laws in the South shared some similarities. "Ultimately, it is the survival of the collectivity that is at stake," said Quebec's minister of justice in defence of Bill 101. "Ours are the institutions which are at stake," said the Alabama Southern Rights firebrand William

Lowndes Yancey in 1860; "ours is the property that is to be destroyed; ours is the honor at stake."[18] "If Montreal is left to so-called bilingualism," declared Professor Léon Dion of Université Laval, "this means in less than ten years a kind of English unilingualism." If Georgia remained in the Union after Lincoln's election, wrote a secessionist in that state, "in TEN years or less our CHILDREN will be the *slaves* of negroes."[19] "When will you English Canadians get it through your thick collective skull that we want to live in a French society, inside and outside, at work and at play, in church and in school," wrote Daniel Latouche in 1990. The South left the Union, said Jefferson Davis in 1861, because Lincoln's election had made "property in slaves so insecure as to be comparatively worthless... thereby annihilating in effect property worth thousands of millions of dollars.... All we ask is to be let alone."[20]

Francophones and Southerners before 1860 also operated in a similar fashion to protect their special interests through their leverage in the dominant national political parties. From 1801 to 1861, the Jeffersonian Republican party and its successor, the Democratic party, controlled the U.S. government most of the time. The core of these parties' strength was in the Slave States, which consistently furnished the votes that enabled them to elect their presidential candidate and a majority of Congress. A Southern slaveholder was president during two-thirds of those years, while most of the Speakers of the House, presidents *pro tem* of the Senate, and Supreme Court justices also came from the Slave States — despite their diminishing percentage of the American population. Similarly, the core strength of the Liberal party in Canada has usually been located in Quebec, which has furnished Canada's prime ministers during most of the past half-century, despite that province's diminishing minority of the Canadian population.

This remarkable political leverage enabled the South and Quebec to win important concessions and legislation at the federal level. In 1850, Southern pressure secured a Fugitive Slave Act. In 1854, Southern Democrats called in their chips to force Senator Stephen A. Douglas to include in the Kansas–Nebraska Act a provision repealing an earlier prohibition of slavery in territories north of 36°30', thereby opening Kansas territory to slavery. With the *Dred Scott* decision in 1857, the Southern majority on the Supreme Court legalized slavery in all federal territories.

An important motive for Northern Democrats to support this legislation and the *Dred Scott* decision was a desire to deter Southern separatism. Similarly, the Liberal party in Canada under Pierre Elliott Trudeau's leadership enacted legislation requiring bilingualism in many spheres of public and commercial life, and gave Quebec special controls over its pension fund, taxing powers, and immigration policy that were not granted to other provinces. In both the ante-bellum United States and in modern Canada, the purpose of these measures was to dampen secessionist fires in the minority regions.

For some Southerners, however, the legislative and judicial victories they won in the 1850s did not go far enough, for they could be reversed by a future Congress or Court if the government fell under Northern antislavery control. The foremost Southern Rights advocate until his death in 1850 was John C. Calhoun. Fearing that the growing Northern majority would eventually destroy the South's distinct society, Calhoun developed an elaborate plan for constitutional revision to establish a dual sovereignty of Free and Slave States by requiring a president to be elected from each section and to have veto power over national legislation. By this means, said Calhoun, the South would regain "the power she possessed of protecting herself before the equilibrium between the sections was destroyed."[21] Calhoun labelled his proposal for dual sovereignty a "concurrent majority." If it or something like it was not soon implemented, he warned, the South would have no choice but to secede in order to protect her distinct society.

Calhoun's concurrent majority bears more than a passing resemblance to René Lévesque's "sovereignty association," which would, in effect, have created dual sovereignties in Quebec and the rest of Canada. Sovereignty association went down to defeat in a referendum in 1980 because most voters in Quebec were not yet prepared to go this far, just as most Southerners were not ready in 1850 to embrace the quasi-independence outlined by Calhoun. Like Pierre Trudeau in Quebec, such Southern leaders as Jefferson Davis preferred to continue exerting leverage through the national Democratic party to protect Southern interests.

But this effort would require concessions by Northern political leaders and voters to help Southerners recapture fugitive slaves in the North, to recognize and protect slavery in Kansas and other territories through a federal slave code, and to annex Cuba as an additional Slave State. By the mid-1850s, most Northern voters were fed up with making further concessions to the South. Building on the foundations laid earlier by the Liberty and Free Soil parties, the Republican party emerged in 1856, only two years after its birth, as the majority party in the Free States and the second-largest party in the country as a whole. Its mushroom growth completed the destruction of the Whig party and crippled the American party.

Republicans opposed any more appeasement of the "Slave Power." The party's greatest strength lay in New England and the northern tier of the Midwest. Again, any similarity to Canadian politics is more than coincidental. In Canada the rise of the Reform Party, whose greatest strength lies in the provinces farthest from Quebec, has been fuelled, in part, by opposition to any more concessions to the francophone majority there. And like the Republicans in the 1850s, the Reform Party has become the majority party in part of Canada, dealing a crippling blow to the Progressive Conservatives and the New Democrats. The polarization in Parliament between the Reform Party, on the one hand, and the Bloc Québécois, on the other, resembles the conflict in Congress between Republicans and Southern

Rights Democrats by 1860. And while it may stretch the comparison too far, one can detect some similarities between the failure of the Crittenden Compromise and other proposals for compromise to forestall Southern secession in 1860–61 and the failure of the Meech Lake and Charlottetown Accords in 1990 and 1992.

There the similarities stop, for the time being at least. No parallel exists between the election of Abraham Lincoln and of Jean Chrétien; just the opposite, in fact. And no Fort Sumter looms on the horizon in Quebec at present. Deep-seated tensions remain, however. One of the most important is what two Canadian scholars, Kenneth McRoberts and Abraham Rotstein, have described as "fundamentally incompatible worldviews" between the Québécois and English Canadians. The "self-image" of the Québécois is "communitarian and integral in its expression," a form of collectivism that emphasizes "*la survivance*" of francophone society as an "organic and coherent" community. In contrast, English Canadians subscribe to values of "egalitarianism and individualism" that emphasize "civil liberties and the classical liberal individualism of Anglo-Saxon cultures."[22]

Similar contrasts between Northern and

Southern worldviews existed in the mid-nineteenth-century United States. Northerners believed in the ideals of egalitarian individualism and competitive meritocracy. "Most Southern whites," however, "regarded themselves less as individuals than as representatives of families that extended through time from the distant past to unborn generations," according to historian Paul Johnson. "Southern life was not about freedom, individual fulfillment, or social progress," which were Northern ideals, but "about honoring the obligations to which one was born."[23]

The corporate, organic conception of Quebec society manifests itself in the form of ethnic nationalism. When anglophone critics branded Quebec's language laws as ethnocentric, Quebec's minister of culture replied unabashedly: "All nations are founded on the principle of ethnocentricity."[24] Ironically, the modern Canadian who most emphatically disagrees with this expression of ethnic nationalism is a native of Quebec: Pierre Trudeau. When Trudeau patriated the Canadian constitution in 1982, he made a Charter of Rights and Freedoms the basis of Canada's definition of itself as a nation. "The Trudeau vision of Canada gave birth to a rival [civic] nationalist ideology to that of

Quebec [ethnic] nationalism," in the words of the Canadian political scientist Peter Russell. "At the core of the Trudeau vision were individual rights — liberal democratic rights and bilingual language rights.... Equal enjoyment of these rights," not corporate ethnic identity, "should be the primary bond of citizenship in the Canadian nation-state."[25] Trudeau opposed the Meech Lake Accord because its "distinct society" clause for Quebec contravened his understanding of the Charter of Rights. "The crucial importance of the Charter," Trudeau declared, meant "that we all share a set of common values and that all Canadians are thence on an equal footing; whether they be Quebecers, Albertans, French, English, Jewish, Hindu, they all have the same rights. No one is special. All Canadians are equal, and that equality flows from the Charter."[26]

The outcome of this struggle between rival visions of Canadian nationalism remains uncertain. Nearly a century and a half ago, the United States experienced its own conflict between ethnic and civic nationalism. An analysis of that contest may reflect some light northward across the 45th parallel.

CHAPTER TWO:
ETHNIC VERSUS CIVIC NATIONALISM IN THE AMERICAN CIVIL WAR

IN RESPONSE TO THE FIRING on Fort Sumter in April 1861 by the army of the newly formed Confederate States of America, President Abraham Lincoln called out the militia to suppress an insurrection. This action forced the Slave States that had not yet seceded to make a choice. Which nation would they support: the United States or the Confederate States? Most citizens of Virginia, North Carolina, Tennessee, and Arkansas did not hesitate; they chose the Confederacy. We must go with "our Southern brothers," declared the Governor of

Tennessee. "Blood is thicker than water," echoed a North Carolina newspaper editor.[1] The Attorney General of Virginia chimed in with an assertion that Virginians were "homogeneous with the [people of the Confederate] States in race," while the Northern people were an "alien race.... The cotton States swarm with Virginia's sons and her son's sons.... They are bone of our bone, and flesh of our flesh." A Louisianian welcomed these "sister States" of the upper South. "This homogeneity will keep us a unit for... much longer than the governments that surround us."[2]

At the same time, Northern leaders insisted that legitimization of the Confederacy would destroy not merely the Union, but the very foundations on which the American nation had been built. That nation "has been consecrated by the blood of our fathers, by the glories of the past, and by the hopes of the future," said outgoing President James Buchanan. If it could be broken by the will of one state or several, the great experiment of republican government launched in 1776 would be proved a failure. "Our example for more than eighty years would not only be lost," Buchanan lamented, "but it would be quoted as conclusive proof that man is unfit for self-government." The incoming president,

Abraham Lincoln, also defined "the central idea pervading this struggle" as the necessity "of proving that popular government is not an absurdity. We must settle this question now, whether in a free government the minority have the right to break up the government whenever they choose. If we fail it will go far to prove the incapability of the people to govern themselves."[3]

Northern newspapers made the same point. A Philadelphia editor declared in June 1861 that "we are fighting to preserve our republican institutions...to establish the authority of the Constitution and laws over violence and anarchy... [and for the] great fundamental principle of republican Government — the right of the majority to rule." By the Confederate attack on the American flag at Fort Sumter, said an Indianapolis newspaper, "the Nation has been deficd. The National Government has been assailed. If either can be done with impunity...we are not a Nation, and our Government is a sham."[4]

The quotations in the preceding three paragraphs frame the competing forms of Confederate and Union nationalism in the American Civil War. They correspond in many ways to the two principal categories of nationalism in the modern world:

ethnic nationalism and civic nationalism. Like all
large concepts, these terms are difficult to define
with precision. The temptation is to take the position of Associate Justice Potter Stewart of the United
States Supreme Court on pornography: while he
couldn't define it, he knew it when he saw it.

Ethnic nationalism is a concept that is probably
easier to grasp. We see it all around us in the world
today. It broke up Yugoslavia into Slovenia, Croa-
tia, Serbia, and Bosnia, and sparked a violent conflict among these ethnic nations. It shattered the
Soviet Union into a bewildering chequerboard of
ethnic nations and led to an ugly, vicious conflict in
Chechnya. It split Czechoslovakia into two nations.
It threatens to do the same to Canada. Basque
nationalism keeps Spain on edge. Kurdish nationalists fight in vain to carve their own nation from por-
tions of Turkey, Iraq, and Iran. Tutsis and Hutu
massacre one another in Rwanda and Burundi,
while, on a smaller scale, Protestants and Catholics
do the same in Northern Ireland in conflicts that are
as much tribal and religious as they are nationalist,
but clearly partake of ethnic nationalism. Readers
will be able to think of a good many other examples
in the contemporary world. Even in the United
Kingdom, the British government has recognized

ethnic nationalism by devolving a degree of sovereign power to the Scottish and Welsh parliaments.

From these examples and from the work of numerous scholars who have studied nationalism, we can derive a definition of ethnic nationalism as the sense of national identity and loyalty shared by a group of people united among themselves and distinguished from others by one or more of the following factors: language; religion; culture; and, most important, a belief in the common genetic or biological descent of the group. Some of these criteria are objective (language and religion), but the last one, in particular, is quite subjective. As one scholar notes, because "there are very few groups in the world today whose members can lay any claim to a known common [genetic] origin, it is not actual descent that is considered essential to the definition of an ethnic group but a belief in a common descent."[5] This points up an essential element in any kind of nationalism, ethnic or otherwise: it is self-defined. As two other noted scholars put it, nationalism "is first and foremost a state of mind, an act of consciousness"; it "is subjective and consists of the self-identification of people with a group."[6]

Several modern students of nationalism maintain that ethnic nationalism is the only authentic kind. They note that the English word "nation" comes from the Latin *nasci* (to be born) or *natio* (the thing born), and that the English word "ethnic" comes from the Greek *ethnos* — which means "nation." Many modern nations, of course, consist of two or more ethnic groups. The United States and Canada are prominent examples. But, strictly speaking, according to political scientist Walker Connor, these are not nations, but rather multi-nation *states*. In his definition, a nation is "a self-differentiating ethnic group...which shares a common ideology, common institutions and customs, and a sense of homogeneity," while a state is "a legal concept describing a social group that occupies a defined territory and is organized under common political institutions and an effective government."[7] The most powerful sentiments of nationalism, in Connor's definition, occur when the state is constituted entirely of a single ethnic nation, as in the cases of Germany and Japan in the 1930s. (These examples are scarcely comforting.) Territorial states that contain one or more self-defining minority ethnic nations within their borders are vulnerable to fragmentation, as in the cases of the former parts of Yugoslavia, the former Soviet Union, and the former Czechoslovakia. Professor Guy Laforest of

Université Laval thinks Canada may share the same fate because, "in English Canada, the state created the nation. The opposite is true of French Canada."[8]

One can scarcely gainsay the potential for ethnic nationalism to break up nation-states. But need we accept the inevitability of this outcome in democratic multi-ethnic nation-states? Need we concede that ethnic identity is the only genuine form of nationalism? Surely not. The United States, Canada, Britain, France, and Belgium — to name some obvious examples — have endured as nation-states for a considerable length of time. What binds their people together is *civic* nationalism. How does one define this? It is the collective identity of a group of people born or living in a specified territory with a shared history, and owing allegiance to a sovereign government whose powers are defined and delimited by laws enacted and enforced through institutions such as Parliament or Congress that evoke a common loyalty to powerful symbols and myths of nationality. "According to the civic nationalist creed," writes one student of nationalism, "what holds a society together is not common roots but law."[9] What defines an American or Canadian or Briton is not ethnic identity, but citizenship. Just as, for Pierre Trudeau, Canadian nationalism is embodied in the Charter of Rights, for Americans the origins of their civic nationalism can be traced, not to descent from an ancient bloodline, but to the Declaration of Independence, the Founding Fathers of 1776, the flag, the Constitution, and the shared history of a victorious struggle for independent nationhood.

One of the best definitions of civic nationalism was offered by Charles Sumner, the radical Republican senator from Massachusetts during the era of the American Civil War, in an address entitled "Are We a Nation?" delivered in 1867. Sumner admitted that the Latin root of the English word "nation" meant that "it was originally applied to a race or people of common descent and language, but seems to have had no reference to a common government. In the latter sense it is modern. Originally ethnological, it is now political." Sumner quoted with approval the definition of "nation" in the French *Dictionary of the Academy*: "The totality of persons born or naturalized in a country and living under the same government." Such a definition "contemplate[s] political unity, rather than unity of blood or language" as the cement of nationalism. "If the inhabitants are of one blood and one language, the unity is more complete," Sumner conceded, "but the essential condition is one sovereignty, involving of course one citizenship." The motto of the United States, *E pluribus unum* — out of many, one — was a succinct definition of civic nationalism. The many and one applied originally to the diverse states that came together to form a nation, but, by the time of Sumner's address, they also applied to the diverse ethnic groups that had become part of the single American nation.[10]

Almost from its founding, the United States was a multi-ethnic nation. Although English language, law, and culture predominated, nearly two-fifths of the white population in 1790 came from non-English stock: Scots, Irish, Germans, Dutch, French, and other European groups. Even if the Scots and Irish are grouped with the English, more than one-fifth of the American white population were non-British. That percentage increased over time, with heavy immigration of non-British peoples, especially after 1840. American civic nationalism became identified not only with citizenship, but also with ideals of liberty, republicanism, manhood suffrage, equality of opportunity, and the absence of rigid class lines. Americans defined their nationality in accordance with these ideals, not in accordance with their ethnic origins. As a Norwegian immigrant wrote to a friend back home: "I have learned to love the country to which I emigrated more sincerely than my old fatherland. I feel free and independent among a free people, who are not chained down by any class or caste systems." This immigrant's choice of words defined the difference between ethnic nationalism ("my old fatherland") and civic nationalism ("a free people...not chained down").[11]

Some European observers, aware of the intensifying ethnic nationalism on their own continent, predicted that the civic nationalism of Americans would eventually splinter along ethnic lines. Alexis de Tocqueville, the most astute ante-bellum European analyst of American society, wrote in 1835 that, "until men have changed their nature and been completely transformed, I shall refuse to believe in the duration of a government which is called upon to hold together forty different nations covering an area half that of Europe, to avoid all rivalry, ambition, and struggles between them, and to unite all their independent wills in the accomplishment of common designs."[12]

But most Americans remained confident of their ability to absorb European nationalit*ies* into American civic nationalit*y*. Herman Melville wrote in 1849 that "there is something in the contemplation of the mode in which America has been settled, that, in a noble breast, should forever extinguish the prejudices of national dislikes. Settled by the people of all nations, all nations may claim her for their own.... Our ancestry is lost in the universal paternity."[13]

There was one glaring exception to the voluntary citizenship that was the centrepiece of American civic nationalism: the slaves. The *Dred Scott* decision in 1857 even declared that free blacks, as the descendants of slaves, were not citizens. One-seventh of the population was thus defined out of American nationality. This egregious violation of civic nationalism helped fuel the antislavery movement. "The monstrous injustice of slavery," said Abraham Lincoln in 1854, "deprives our republican example of its just influence in the world" and "enables the enemies of free institutions, with plausibility, to taunt us as hypocrites."[14]

For a time in the 1850s, the sentiment known as "nativism" also threatened to breach American civic nationalism and push it in the direction of ethnic nationalism. Nativists were those American-born Protestants who resented the large influx of Irish and German Catholic immigrants in the 1840s and 1850s. Organized in secret lodges, they were instructed to tell outsiders who asked about these societies: "I know nothing." Hence they were called "Know-Nothings." In 1854 they founded the American party and went into politics. The goals of this party were to limit the influence of foreign-born men in politics and to lengthen the waiting period for immigrants to become naturalized citizens from five to twenty-one years.

Although some leaders of the other political party born in 1854, the Republican party, were tempted to form an alliance with the Know-Nothings, most opposed this "organized scheme of bigotry and proscription" as an "indelible shame of our politics," in the words of a founder of the Republican party in Indiana. Since "we are against Black Slavery, because the slaves are deprived of human rights," declared other Republicans, "we are also against [this] system of Northern Slavery to be created by disfranchising Irish and Germans."[15] The most prominent foreign-born Republican, Carl Schurz, attacked nativism as a mockery of the civic nationalism of the Founding Fathers, "whose mother-country was the world" and who "establish[ed] the *Republic of equal rights, where the title of manhood is the title to citizenship*." It was Lincoln who offered the clearest indictment of nativism as contrary to the ideals of civic nationalism. "Our progress in degeneracy appears to me to be pretty rapid," he wrote in 1855. "As a nation, we began by declaring that 'all men are created equal.' We now practically read it 'all men are created equal, *except negroes.*' When the Know-Nothings get control, it will read 'all men are created equal, except negroes, *and foreigners, and catholics.*' When it comes to this I should prefer emigrating to some country where they make no pretence of loving liberty — to Russia, for instance, where despotism can be taken pure, and without the base alloy of hypocracy [*sic*]."[16]

By 1860 the looming crisis of civil war had driven nativism into the shadows, from which it has periodically emerged to challenge the tenets of civic nationalism. The real threat to American nationalism, however, came not from nativists or their immigrant adversaries, but from Southern nationalism. At first glance it may seem perverse to describe this phenomenon as ethnic nationalism. Southern whites shared the same language with other Americans, the same Christian and mainly Protestant religion, the same predominantly British heritage, a common memory of the struggle for independent nationhood, and a common allegiance to the Constitution and the political institutions that had grown up under it, which they had played a major role in shaping.

Yet these commonalities coexisted with a widespread and growing impression that Northern and Southern whites were two peoples with increasingly hostile interests. As a student at Harvard from 1817 to 1821, Ralph Waldo Emerson knew several Southern students and reflected on "the peculiar and striking distinctions which we see at Cambridge separating our Northern and Southern countrymen." A New Yorker travelling in the South in 1844 commented that "life is so different from that at the North...I felt that I was indeed a stranger in a strange land."[17] Southern visitors to the North reciprocated that sentiment. One of them described the North as "a totally alien country"; another wrote in 1854 from Boston that "I feel as an alien." In 1861 the son of a wealthy Georgia planter, Charles C. Jones, Jr., who had graduated from Princeton and from Harvard Law School, described Northern and Southern whites as "two races which, although claiming a common parentage, have been so entirely separated by climate, by morals, by religion, and by estimates so totally opposite of all that constitutes honor, truth, and manliness, that they cannot longer coexist under the same government.

Oil and water will not commingle.... The sooner we separate the better."[18]

European travellers in the United States echoed these observations. Tocqueville commented on the "marked differences" between Northerners and Southerners who had "sprung from the same stock."[19] A Scottish visitor described Southerners as "quite a distinct race from the 'Yankees,'" while an Englishman added that South Carolina planters despised Northerners as "an inferior race of men.... There is nothing a Southern man resents so much as to be called a Yankee."[20]

By the eve of the Civil War, according to Congressman Alfred Iverson of Georgia, there was "an enmity between the northern and southern people that is deep and enduring, and you never can eradicate it — never!... I believe that the northern people hate the South worse than ever the English people hated France."[21] The famous correspondent of the *Times* of London, William Howard Russell, found on his travels in the South in early 1861 "a degree of something like ferocity in the Southern mind towards New England which exceeds belief." William Gilmore Simms, the South's leading novelist, and editor of the *Southern Quarterly Review* in the 1850s, described the South as "a people, a nation" possessing such different "national characteristics" from the North "in essential, moral, and physical respects" that its destiny as "a separate political community" was inevitable.[22]

What accounted for this hostility between peoples who, as Tocqueville noted, had "sprung from the same stock"? Tocqueville's own answer was that "almost all the marked differences in character between northerners and southerners have their roots in slavery."[23] Indeed, the peculiar institution was the wedge that split the two sections farther and farther apart. William H. Seward, in 1858, described an "irrepressible conflict" between rival social orders founded upon slave labour and free labour. It was this conflict, said Abraham Lincoln the same year, that made the United States a house divided against itself.[24] In March 1861, the new vice-president of the Confederacy, Alexander Stephens of Georgia, said in a speech at Savannah that the conflict over slavery was "the immediate cause" of secession. Stephens pronounced one of the charters of American civic nationalism, the Declaration of Independence, with its ringing affirmation that all men are created equal, to be false. "Our new government is founded on exactly the opposite idea," said Stephens. "Its cornerstone rests upon the great truth that the negro is not equal to the white man; that slavery...is his natural and moral condition. This, our new Government, is the first in the history of the world, based on this great physical, philosophical, and moral truth."[25]

That the slavery controversy was the main cause of secession is a truism. But was Stephens's declaration of white supremacy an expression of ethnic nationalism? Not precisely; though it was related to the Southern consciousness of ethnic distinctiveness in both obvious and subtle ways. The Scottish traveller who referred to Southerners as a "distinct race from the 'Yankees,'" however, and Charles C. Jones, Jr., who described Northerners and Southerners as "two races," were not referring to Caucasian and Negro. They meant that Northern and Southern *whites* belonged to distinctive ethnic groups — or races, as ethnic groups were usually described in the nineteenth century. That is also what the North Carolina editor meant when he declared that his state must join the Confederacy: the blood ties among people of the Slave States were thicker than their watery ties of civic nationalism to the people of the Free States.

The origins of ethnic nationalism in the nineteenth century lay in the response by German intellectuals and cultural leaders to the French revolution and to Napoleon's conquests in the first decade of that century. They created a notion of the German *Volk* whose blood ties should unite all Germans against the French tyrant. This concept of the *Volk* grew more and more powerful until Otto von Bismarck, who urged Germans to "think with your blood," united most German-speaking peoples into a single state in 1871. Ethnic nationalism became the hallmark of nineteenth-century European romanticism. It was a top-down creation, an archetype constructed by intellectuals and diffused into the culture through literature, music, art, and eventually political discourse, to support the struggles of Greeks, Hungarians, Poles, Norwegians, and other ethnic nationalities for independent nationhood.[26]

By 1860, Southern nationalists could draw not only on these traditions, but also on those closer to their own culture. The extraordinary popularity in the South of Sir Walter Scott's novels can be explained, in part, by Southern resonance with Scott's romantic portrayal of Scotland's efforts to express its cultural nationalism *vis-à-vis* England. Southerners acquired the term "Southron" from Scott. This was an archaic Scottish word for Southerner, meaning the English people on Scotland's border.

Whether aware of the irony or not, Southern whites transposed this vaguely contemptuous Scottish word into a term of Southern pride to distinguish themselves from "Yankees."

An even greater irony inhered in the particular popularity in the South of Scott's novel *Ivanhoe*. Set in the twelfth century, the novel portrays a struggle between descendants of Norman conquerors and the vanquished Anglo-Saxons for the soul of England. Most of Scott's Norman protagonists are cruel, arrogant, and overbearing, while the novel's hero and heroine, Ivanhoe and Rowena, are Anglo-Saxons. Southern readers seem to have missed the main point. Their enthusiasm for the novel coincided with the rise of the central myth of Southern ethnic nationalism: the idea that Southern whites, or at least the planter class, were descended from the English Cavaliers of the seventeenth century, who in turn were descended from the Normans, while Yankees were descended from the "Saxon churls" by way of the seventeenth-century Puritans who migrated to New England when the Cavaliers migrated to Virginia.

This belief gained a remarkable currency among the Southern cultural elite. By 1860 it had become diffused into the discourse of Southern nationalism.

One of the fullest expressions of this ethnic nationalism appeared in the *Southern Literary Messenger* in June 1860, just as the crucial presidential election campaign was warming up. Published in Richmond, the *Messenger* was the principal outlet for Southern writers. This article boldly declared the sectional conflict to be "a contest of race...between the North and the South.... The people of the Northern States are more immediately descended of the English Puritans" who "constituted as a class the common people of England...and were descended of the ancient Britons and Saxons.... The Southern States were settled and governed...by...persons belonging to...that stock recognized as Cavaliers...directly descended from the Norman Barons of William the Conqueror, a race distinguished in its earliest history for its warlike and fearless character, a race in all times since renowned for its gallantry, chivalry, honor, gentleness, and intellect.... The Southern people come of that race."[27]

The South's leading writer on political economy, James B.D. De Bow, subscribed to this Norman–Cavalier thesis and helped to popularize it in his influential journal published in New Orleans, *De Bow's Review*. As the lower-South states seceded one after another during the winter of 1860–61, *De*

Bow's Review carried several long articles justifying this separation on the grounds of irreconcilable ethnic differences between Southern and Northern whites. "The Cavaliers, Jacobites, and Huguenots, who settled the South, naturally hate, contemn, and despise the Puritans who settled the North," proclaimed one such article written by George Fitzhugh, the South's foremost pro-slavery intellectual. "The former are a master-race — the latter a slave race, the descendants of Saxon serfs.... Cavaliers and Jacobites are of Norman descent, and the Normans were of Roman descent, and so were the Huguenots. The Saxons and Angles, ancestors of the Yankees, came from the cold and marshy regions of the North, where man is little more than a cold-blooded, amphibious biped."[28]

De Bow's Review proudly contrasted the South's ethnic nationalism with the civic nationalism of the North. "The two distinct peoples" of North and South, another article declared, had been forced into an alliance in 1776 by the common cause against Britain. But the Union they formed was an experiment doomed to failure. "The Roundhead and the Cavalier that had crossed swords under the hostile banners of Fairfax and Rupert, met again, on American soil; and when the battle was fought, in the [constitutional] convention of 1787," the Round-heads prevailed in the adoption of a constitution with inadequate protections for the institution of slavery. "The dissolution of the American Union was written in the Declaration of Independence, and foreshadowed in every provision of the Constitution," insisted the author. "The two civilizations never had anything in common but mutual hatreds and antipathies, even during that period when their blood mingled in one stream, on every battle-field." The South was now recovering its "independent destiny" by repudiating the failed experiment of civic nationalism that had sought "to erect one nation out of two irreconcilable peoples."[29]

These ideas percolated into the Southern popular press, and even affected outsiders. As early as 1835, the French King Louis-Philippe wrote to Charles Gayarré of New Orleans, an American of French descent, that "you have the Puritans in the North and the Cavaliers in the South, Democracy with its leveling rod, and Aristocracy with slavery raising its haughty head in the other section and creating a social elegance, a superiority of breeding, and race." A visitor from Michigan to Mississippi in the 1850s described the sectional conflict as one pitting "the Saxon North against the Norman South."

A Louisville newspaper acknowledged that, until Lincoln's election, the South had controlled the national government just as "our Norman kinsmen in England, always a minority, have ruled their Saxon countrymen." The South departed when Lincoln came in, this editorial continued, because "the Norman Cavalier of the South cannot brook the vulgar familiarity of the Saxon Yankee."[30] The Richmond *Daily Dispatch*, with the largest circulation of any newspaper in the Confederacy, published frequent editorials analysing "the incongruous and discordant elements out of which the framers of the Constitution sought to create a homogeneous people.... The great wonder is not that the two sections have fallen asunder at last, but that they held together so long.... The dissimilarity between moral constitutions, habits of thought, breeding and manners of the Cavalier and Roundhead must necessarily run in the blood for generations, and defy all the glue and cement of political unions." And the Confederacy's poet laureate, Henry Timrod, celebrated the formal creation of the Confederate States of America as "a nation among nations" in a poem with the significant title "Ethnogenesis."[31]

The Richmond *Daily Dispatch* insisted that, "even if slavery had never existed," the American descendants of Cavaliers and Puritans "would have gone to war, sooner or later.... The Roundhead has more reason than ever to feel that the Cavalier is his superior, and...that galling fact, eating into his bones, would have rendered perpetual peace between the two [sections] impossible."[32] Nevertheless, proponents of the Norman–Cavalier thesis readily incorporated slavery into their ideology. After all, the Normans were a ruling race, and therefore had "an affinity with the institution of slavery," according to articles in the *Southern Literary Messenger* and *De Bow's Review*. By contrast, the subordinate Saxons — who became Yankees — did not possess "that combination of dignified greatness and natural command, so necessary to the proper control of slavery." As a consequence, the Yankees developed "an insane philanthropy for the negro," while the "conservative, bold, chivalrous, and commanding" Norman Southrons, with "their peculiar capacity for *executive control*," were "the only people on this continent who can properly control... this particular institution of slavery." Thus it became "the mission of the Norman blood of this country" to exercise "the power and charm of slavery."[33]

The Norman–Cavalier thesis, on the face of it, seems little short of ludicrous. Indeed, modern scholars have shown it to have scarcely any foundation in fact. Few Southerners in 1860 were descended from Cavaliers, and even fewer Cavaliers could claim unmixed descent from the Norman barons of William the Conqueror.[34] But these facts are irrelevant to a consideration of ethnic nationalism. As virtually every student of this phenomenon has noted, ethnic nationalism is much more a subjective than an objective reality; it is an "invented tradition," an "imagined community," an instrumental construction of a genealogy to serve cultural or political ends.[35] "Nationality is born of the decision to form a nationality," writes one historian; "what ultimately matters," according to another, "is not *what is* but *what people believe is.*" As a French scholar of nationalism noted more than a century ago: "Getting its history wrong is part of being a nation."[36]

American civic nationalism also constructed symbols and myths to promote a sense of nationhood. The most potent of those symbols were associated with the generation that had invented the republic in 1776, won its independence in 1783, and formed its government in 1789. In the eyes of most Northerners, the break-up of the Union by Southern secession threatened to destroy all the achievements of this heroic generation. In an editorial published soon after the Confederate attack on Fort Sumter, a Vermont newspaper expressed the sentiments of civic nationalism shared by millions of Yankees. "What is Our Government Worth?" asked the title of the editorial, which proceeded to answer: "If one wishes to have even a faint idea of what this government cost, let him go to Lexington and Concord, to [Bunker] Hill and Saratoga... Bennington and Yorktown... where the blood of our fathers flowed like water, as the price which was paid not simply for our liberty, but chiefly for our *Law*, for our *Government*." When the issue is "Government or no Government — Law or no Law, Liberty or Anarchy — let there be no questioning as to 'What is all this worth?'... It is more to us than houses or lands or commerce... more than life itself, for in its preservation and permanence, these all have protection and security and continue to be blessings beyond price."[37]

No one invoked these emblems of civic nationalism more frequently or effectively than Abraham Lincoln. On his way to Washington in February 1861, the president-elect addressed the New Jersey legislature in Trenton, near the spot where George Washington's ragged troops won a victory the day after Christmas 1776 that saved the Revolution from collapse. "There must have been something more than common that those men struggled for," said Lincoln. "I am exceedingly anxious that this Union, the Constitution, and the liberties of the people shall be perpetuated in accordance with the original idea for which that struggle was made." Next day, Washington's Birthday, Lincoln spoke at Independence Hall in Philadelphia. "It was not the mere matter of the separation of the colonies from the mother land" that Americans fought for in 1776, he declared, "but that sentiment in the Declaration of Independence which gave liberty, not only to the people of this country, but hope for the world...that in due time the weights should be lifted from the shoulders of all men, and that *all* should have an equal chance." Ten days later, in the peroration of his inaugural address, Lincoln expressly invoked the heritage of civic nationalism in an appeal to Southerners: "We are not enemies, but friends. We must not be enemies. Though passion may have strained, it must not break our bonds of affection. The mystic chords of memory, stretching from every battle-field, and patriot grave, to every living heart and hearthstone, all over this broad land, will yet swell the chorus of the Union, when again touched, as surely they will be, by the better angels of our nature."[38]

Lincoln knew what he was doing in this entreaty. Southerners had been equal partners in the founding of the nation, and senior partners in its administration during most of its four-score years. Many Confederates were of divided minds in 1861. One part of that mind wanted to establish a separate existence from the hated "Yankees," whom they portrayed as a different and inferior "race." The other part gloried in the shared legacy of 1776 "stretching from every battle-field and patriot grave." In an attempt to capture the legacy exclusively for the Confederacy, many Southern leaders insisted that, with Lincoln's election, the North had corrupted the original purpose of the Revolution and the Constitution, which the Confederacy would restore by its own revolution for independence. In his first message to the Confederate Congress after the war began, Jefferson Davis urged Southerners to "renew such sacrifices as our fathers made to the holy cause of constitutional liberty." The Confederate Constitution replicated verbatim most parts of the U.S. Constitution. The great seal of the Confederacy portrayed George Washington, while Confederate money and postage stamps bore the portraits of Washington, Thomas Jefferson, Andrew Jackson, and other heroes of the American pantheon. A Confederate songbook contained a stirring tune that linked the two American revolutions, titled "Seventy-Six and Sixty-One."[39]

Southern nationalists, however, recognized the danger that this lingering affection for the mythic memories of *American* nationalism might seduce hesitant secessionists from their Confederate allegiance, as Lincoln sought to do. Once the Civil War began, therefore, many Southern opinion-makers redoubled their efforts to distance their people ethnically from the Yankees. Dozens of editorials and articles in Confederate magazines and newspapers rang the changes on this theme. "The present conflict in America is not a *civil* strife, but a war of *Nationalities*," insisted a Louisiana writer, "a war of alien races....Cavalier and Roundhead no longer designate parties, but *nations*, whose separate foundations were laid on Plymouth Rock and the banks of the James River." Those Virginia Cavaliers "became the august mother of that beautiful sisterhood of States, dwelling in the bosom of the Mississippi valley, and stretching along the shores of the Mexican gulf." This "warrior race will found an empire, illustrious in arms, as renowned in arts, and show the Cavalier blood to be still worthy of its Norman origin." When the *"inferior race"* of Saxon Yankees was "whipped, and *well whipped*" the "Norman race [will] record, in America, what, with strong hand and ten centuries of dominion and power, it has written on the civilization of Europe."[40]

By 1863, a Virginian writing in the *Southern Literary Messenger* could claim a "broad and irrefutable" consensus in the South that "the Saxonized maw-worms, creeping from the Mayflower on to the cold, forbidding crags of the North, have [no] right to kinship with the whole-souled Norman British planters of a gallant race, on a welcoming sunny soil of the South."[41] This consensus found its way into Confederate poetry and song, as in this verse from "Southrons' Chaunt of Defiance":

> You have no such blood as ours
> > For the shedding;
> In the veins of cavaliers
> > Was its heading![42]

As the Northern war effort escalated to a no-holds-barred campaign to destroy Confederate resources and property, including slavery, Southern writers added a new wrinkle to their depiction of Yankees as barbarous latter-day Saxons and Puritans. "The brutal, cruel, greedy, licentious, hypocritical, and sacreligious Roundheads are alive again in their descendants," declared the Richmond *Daily Dispatch*, "and now threaten to make a St. Domingo of the South." The Anglo-Saxons of England, noted another Southerner, had sprung from the Goths and Vandals, who had destroyed the Roman Empire. By the similar behaviour of Union armies in the South, he concluded, the world now saw how "the terms Goth and Vandal" had been "condensed in the synonyme [*sic*] Yankee."[43]

Indeed, virtually all of the derogatory terms used by Southern journalists, poets, and political leaders, and by Confederate soldiers themselves, to describe the enemy carried ethnic overtones. The Yankees were not only Goths and Vandals; they were also "hordes of Northern Hessians" "as numerous as the swarms of barbarians which the frozen North sent from her loins to overrun the Roman Empire" or as "the hordes of Alaric and Attila."[44] Henry Timrod wrote a Confederate war poem that contained this couplet: "Fling down thy gauntlet to the Huns, / And roar the challenge from the guns."[45] Other Confederate poems included

such lines as: "The North sends a ravenous pack ...
ATTILA, fearful destroyer, Merciless GENGHIS
KHAN"; "What! shall this grovelling race, who
cringe for gold, Make laws for Southern men, on
Southern soil?"; and a description of Yankees as
"Most venal of a venal race."[46]

The term "Yankee" itself carried strong ethnic
overtones similar to such words as "Mick,"
"Polack," "Canuck," "Kike," and so on. And, during the Civil War, Confederate songwriters sometimes lumped the Yankees together with other
ethnic stereotypes of Northerners, as in this mock-
ing song written after the first Battle of Manassas to
the tune of "Yankee Doodle":

> Then forth he went, with bold intent,
>   to gather up his legions —
> A crew of dirty vagabonds, from
>   Tophet's nether regions —
> Of thieving Yankees, filthy Dutch,
>   and Irish from the Bogs.
> And vagrant Hoosiers from the West —
>   a herd of drunken hogs.[47]

Another Confederate ballad portrayed the South as
fighting not only against the Yankees but also

'Gainst the spawn of Europe, and all the lands
British and German — Norway's sands,
Dutchland and Irish — the hireling bands
    Bought for butchery — recking no rede,
But, flocking like vultures, with felon hands,
    To fatten the rage of greed.[48]

An educated sergeant in a Louisiana regiment, a schoolmaster before the war, managed to compare the Yankees with two different ethnic groups when he wrote in 1863 of his "absolute hatred of . . . the hyperborean vandals with whom we are waging a war for existence. . . . The Thugs of India will not bear a comparison of my hatred and destruction of them when opportunity offers. . . . I expect to murder every Yankee I ever meet when I can do so with impunity if I live a hundred years."[49] Such expressions of hatred for the Yankee "race" were common in the letters of Confederate soldiers. "The combined & united power of that mercernary [*sic*] Race that are seeking to subjugate us can never succeed," wrote a Georgia lieutenant to his wife in 1862. "Let the mothers of G[eorgi]a instill from their breast into their infants a bitter & lasting hatred to this Race of people." A Texas captain likewise instructed his wife to teach their children "a

bitter and unrelenting hatred to the Yankee race...
[a] vile and cursed race."[50]

In contrast, Southerners identified themselves
with admired peoples who had struggled for independence. At a low point for the Confederate cause
in the spring of 1862, De Bow compared the plight
of the South to that of ancient Greece against the
Persian hordes of Xerxes. "The soul of the Greek
rose with the danger," declared De Bow. "Let our
spirit be loftier than that of the pagan Greek, and
we can succeed in making every pass a Thermo-
pylae, every strait a Salamis, and every plain a Marathon." A poet picked up this theme with a verse
declaring that "The holy fire that nerved the Greek/
to make his stand at Marathon" would fire the
Southern heart against the Yankees.[51] In "A Poem
for the Times," another Southern versifier warned
the North:

'Twere well to remember this land of the sun
    Is a *nutrix Leonum*, and suckles a race
Strong-armed, lion-hearted and banded as one
    Who brook not oppression and know
        not disgrace....
We greet you, as greeted the Swiss, Charles the Bold,
    With a farewell to peace and a welcome to war.[52]

The nineteenth century furnished Southerners several examples of ethnic-nationalist wars of independence to emulate. When Polish nationalists rose in rebellion against Russian rule in 1863, Confederate newspapers drew the obvious parallel. "At bottom," proclaimed the Richmond *Enquirer*, "the cause of Poland is the same cause for which the Confederates are now fighting ... against that crushing, killing union with another nationality." A year later, the *Enquirer* reaffirmed that, like the Greeks against Turkey, the Hungarians against the Habsburgs, and Poland against Russia, "we are fighting for the idea of race."[53]

In contrast to ethnic terms such as "Hessian" and "Hun" that Southerners used to describe the enemy, Northerners referred to Confederates in pejorative terms consistent with civic nationalism: they were "rebels," "traitors," an arrogant "aristocracy" of "miserable despots who are trying to destroy our country."[54] Northern determination to punish "treason" fuelled a zeal for vengeance equal to the Southern desire for revenge against "hyperborean vandals." As William T. Sherman's army entered South Carolina in 1865, one of the Union soldiers expressed a fierce joy at the chance to punish this "mother of traitors." Another Northern soldier voiced contempt for the self-styled Carolina aristocrats who "can talk of nothing but the purity of blood of themselves & their ancestors.... Their cant about aristocracy is perfectly sickening.... If you hear any condemning us for what we have done, tell them for me and for Sherman's army, that 'we found here the authors of all the calamities that have befallen this nation ... and that their punishment is light when compared with what justice demanded.'"[55]

Northern soldiers also expressed positive and patriotic as well as negative and vengeful motives of civic nationalism. "Our fathers made this country, we their children are to save it," wrote a young Ohio lawyer to his wife who had opposed his enlistment, leaving her and two small children at home. If "our institutions prove a failure and our Country be numbered among the things that were but are not ... of what value would be house, family, and friends?" A British immigrant working in a Philadelphia textile mill explained to his father back in England why he had enlisted in the Union army. "If the Unionists let the South secede," he wrote, "the West might want to follow and this country would be as bad as the German states.... There would have to be another form of a constitution wrote [*sic*] and after it was written who would obey it?"[56]

It was Lincoln who gave direction and shape to these convictions of civic nationalism. "This is essentially a People's contest," he told Congress on the Fourth of July 1861. "It is a struggle for maintaining in the world, that form, and substance of government, whose leading object is...to afford all, an unfettered start, and a fair chance, in the race of life." The issue of the war, Lincoln continued, "embraces more than the fate of these United States. It presents to the whole family of man, the question, whether a constitutional republic, or a democracy, can, or cannot, maintain its territorial integrity."[57]

Lincoln's most eloquent expression of civic nationalism, indeed the best such evocation in American letters, is the Gettysburg Address. This Civil War, said Lincoln at Gettysburg, was the great test whether a nation founded four score and seven years earlier, "conceived in Liberty, and dedicated to the proposition that all men are created equal," could long endure. Lincoln called on his fellow countrymen to dedicate themselves anew to the unfinished work of civic nationalism that those Union soldiers who died at Gettysburg had given their "last full measure of devotion" to achieve: "that government of the people, by the people, for the people, shall *not* perish from the earth."

Northern civilians and soldiers alike took inspiration from Lincoln's words. A British newspaper correspondent covering the American Civil War expressed amazement in 1864 at "the extent and depth of the [Northern] determination to fight to the last.... They are in earnest in a way the like of which the world never saw before, silently, calmly, but desperately in earnest; they will fight on, in my opinion, as long as they have men, muskets, [and] powder...and would fight on, though the grass were growing in Wall Street, and there was not a gold dollar on this side of the Atlantic."[58]

Union soldiers confirmed this prediction. "Sick as I am of this war and bloodshed [and] as much oh how much I want to be home with my dear wife and children," wrote a Pennsylvania officer after fighting for nearly three years, he intended to stay in to the end because "every day I have a more religious feeling, that this war is a crusade for the good of mankind.... I [cannot] bear to think of what my children would be if we were to permit this hell-begotten conspiracy to destroy this country."[59] Justifying to his wife a decision to stay in the army after recovering from a wound instead of accepting a medical discharge, a thirty-three-year-old Minnesota sergeant, father of three children, wrote that "my grandfather fought and risked his life to bequeath to his posterity... the glorious Institutions" now threatened by "this infernal rebellion.... It is not for you and I, or us & our dear little ones, alone, that I was and am willing to risk the fortunes of the battle-field, but also for the sake of the country's millions who are to come after us." When Robert E. Lee finally surrendered at Appomattox, a New Jersey officer who had fought for four years wrote to his wife that he could now come home proud that "it has been our privilege to live and take part in the struggle that has decided for all time to come that Republics are not a failure."[60]

But what of that "monstrous injustice" of slavery that violated the central tenet of civic nationalism — inclusive citizenship? Union victory abolished the institution and brought forth the "new birth of freedom" that Lincoln heralded at Gettysburg. "In *giving* freedom to the slave, we *assure* freedom to the free," Lincoln said on another occasion.[61] In 1868, the Fourteenth Amendment to the Constitution confirmed one of the most important results of the Civil War, and remedied the most blatant defect in American civic nationalism, with the words that "all persons born or naturalized in the United States" are citizens and that no state can "abridge the privileges or immunities of citizens" or "deny to any person within its jurisdiction the equal protection of the laws."

These phrases of the Fourteenth Amendment have had a profound impact on the course of civic nationalism in the United States. They have provided the constitutional basis for desegregation decisions by the Supreme Court and for civil-rights legislation by Congress since the 1950s. They also blunted the recurrent extrusions of ethnic nationalism that sought to deny citizenship to various categories of immigrants, including illegal immigrants, by assuring that their children born in the United States would automatically become citizens.

Victorious Northerners assumed that the Civil War's outcome had destroyed specious Southern claims of ethnic superiority grounded in alleged Norman–Cavalier ancestry. After the fall of Richmond in April 1865, Union Secretary of the Navy Gideon Welles blamed the previous four years of slaughter on "the diseased imagination" of Southerners "who some thirty and forty years since studied Scott's novels, and fancied themselves cavaliers.... They came ultimately to believe themselves a superior and better race, knights of blood and spirit. Only a war could wipe out this arrogance and folly." At a commemoration for Harvard College's war dead on July 21, 1865, James Russell Lowell wrote an ode containing these lines:

Who now shall sneer?
Who dare again to say we trace
Our lines to a plebeian race?
Roundhead and Cavalier![62]

During the Franco-Prussian War in 1870–71, when France claimed to fight for something called the "Latin race" against the Germanic race, the German-born American political scientist Francis Lieber ridiculed the claim as akin to Southern assertions of Norman descent. "Races are very often invented from ignorance, or for evil purposes," wrote Lieber in a passage that seems strikingly modern. "The rebels told us and each other again and again that they were a race totally different from the race of the North." This "pitiful attempt," Lieber declared, consisted of nothing more than "arbitrary maxims, vague conceits, or metaphorical expressions."[63]

Vague and arbitrary or not, such thinking did not disappear in the South. On June 17, 1865, the

seventy-two-year-old Virginian Edmund Ruffin, an
original secessionist who claimed to have fired the
first gun against Fort Sumter, made a final entry in
his diary, vowing "unmitigated hatred ... to the per-
fidious, malignant, & vile Yankee race." He then
put a barrel of a rifle in his mouth and blew out his
brains. Most Southrons did not respond so drasti-
cally to the bitter proof that the illustrious warrior
race descended from Normans could not whip those
churlish Saxon Yankees after all. Rather, they followed the advice of Edward Pollard, wartime editor
of the Richmond *Examiner*. Pollard wrote the first
history of the Confederacy, whose title, *The Lost
Cause*, gave a label to the romantic glorification of
those Cavaliers of 1861–65 that is still with us
today. "There may not be a political South," Pollard admitted in 1868, but there can be "a social
and intellectual South. . . . It would be immeasurably
the worst consequence of defeat in this war that
the South should lose its moral and intellectual
distinctiveness as a people and cease to assert its
well known superiority in civilization ... over the
people of the North." The war may have decided
the questions of slavery and Confederate independence, Pollard conceded, but it "did not decide
negro equality. . . . This new cause — or rather the

true question of the war revived — is the supremacy of the white race."[64]

Despite the outcome of the Civil War, the contest between civic nationalism has not ended — in the United States or elsewhere in the world. At the end of the twentieth century, the words that Lincoln spoke in the middle of the nineteenth are as relevant now with respect to convictions of racial or ethnic superiority as they were then with respect to slavery: they deprive "our republican example of its just influence in the world" and enable "the enemies of free institutions, with plausibility, to taunt us as hypocrites."

EPILOGUE

IN ONE OF HIS MOST STRIKING PASSAGES, the Southern
novelist William Faulkner summed up the Lost Cause
nostalgia that has shaped the *mentalité* of generations
of white Southerners. "For every Southern boy fourteen
years old," wrote Faulkner in *Intruder in the Dust*, "not
once but whenever he wants it, there is the instant
when it's still not yet two o'clock on that July after-
noon in 1863, the brigades are in position behind the rail
fence, the guns are laid and ready in the woods and the
furled flags are already loosened to break out and Pickett

himself with his long oiled ringlets and his hat in one hand probably and his sword in the other looking up the hill waiting for Longstreet to give the word and it's all in the balance, it hasn't happened yet... and that moment doesn't need even a four-teen-year-old boy to think *This time. Maybe this time* with all this much to lose and all this much to gain: Pennsylvania, Maryland, the world, the golden dome of Washington itself to crown with desperate and unbelievable victory the desperate gamble, the cast made two years ago...."[1]

At first glance this bittersweet imagery seems to bear some resemblance to the Québécois mindset that Canadian historian Ramsay Cook has labelled "conquestism." This phenomenon, wrote Cook, "is one of the most important subjects in the intellectual history of French Canada. Each generation of French Canadians appears to fight, intellectually, the battle of the Plains of Abraham all over again."[2] But Québécois conquestism is a far more serious matter than Faulkner's fourteen-year-old boy's fantasy of charging up Cemetery Ridge again with Pickett at Gettysburg. The prospect of Quebec's independence is real; the dream of Confederate independence is a form of ritual pageantry presented by re-enactors who wave the Confederate flag in an elaborate charade of ancestor worship and psychological escapism. Everyone understands that it is romance, not reality. When Robert E. Lee surrendered to Ulysses S. Grant at Appomattox, the United States became one nation, indivisible, in reality as well as theory. Since 1865 no state or region has seriously threatened secession, not even during the "massive resistance" to desegregation by several Southern states from 1954 to 1964. The South is today one of the most patriotic regions of America; many who profess a love for the Confederate flag would be among the first to leap to the defence of the American flag and the civic nationalism it represents.

The death of the Confederate dream of ethnic nationalism does not mean that it was never a serious threat. In a recent commentary on Quebec separatism, the American scholar Michael Walzer wrote: "Given the absence of strong territorially based minorities, the American union has never faced a 'Quebecan' challenge."[3] This statement would come as astonishing news to the three million Americans who fought in the Civil War. Admittedly, Southern whites in 1861 could not lay claim to the same degree of ethnic distinctiveness that Quebeckers can. They spoke the same language as

"Yankees" (even though distinctive accents sometimes made it hard for them to understand each
other) and shared a similar, predominantly British
Protestant heritage. Yet, as noted in the preceding
chapter, all ethnic nationalisms are in some ways an
"invented tradition," an "imagined community,"
but are none the less powerful because of their
imaginary qualities. If the Confederacy's ethnic distinctiveness was largely an artificial creation,
Quebec's distinct society is also partially the creation of state policy that has relentlessly promoted
French language and culture and repressed English
language and culture. And the *pure laine* may not
be quite so pure as many Québécois imagine, given
the cumulative impact of intermarriages between
English and French Canadians over the past eight or
nine generations.

In any event, many Southern whites believed as
strongly in their ethnic difference from Yankees as
the Québécois believe in their ethnic difference from
English Canadians. The percentage of the white
Confederate population killed in the Civil War was
the equivalent of 280,000 Quebeckers, 1,130,000
Canadians, or 10,400,000 Americans killed in a war
fought at the end of the twentieth century. Would
the nationalism, ethnic or civic, of Quebeckers,

Canadians, or Americans today be capable of sustaining such losses? Artificially constructed as it was, Confederate ethnic nationalism was nevertheless powerful.

The triumph of civic nationalism in 1865 meant nothing less than the survival of the *United* States. Americans of that generation understood this truth, even if contemporary scholars like Michael Walzer have forgotten it. In an address at the dedication of the Union soldiers' monument at Gettysburg on July 4, 1869, Indiana's wartime governor, Oliver Morton, reflected on "what would be our condition if the Rebellion had triumphed.... Had the bond of union been broken, the various parts would have crumbled to pieces. We should have a slave-holding confederacy in the South; a republic on the Pacific; another in the Northwest, and another in the East. With the example of one successful secession, dismemberment of the balance would have speedily followed; and our country, once the hope of the world, the pride of our hearts, broken into hostile fragments, would have been blotted from the map, and become a byword among nations."[4]

Morton spoke two years after the British North America Act had created the Dominion of Canada. What Morton celebrated as a challenge surmounted, the architect and first prime minister of Canada echoed as a challenge to be met. "We are a great country," said Sir John A. Macdonald a few years after Morton spoke, "and shall become one of the greatest in the world if we preserve it. We shall sink into insignificance if we permit it to be broken."[5]

Abraham Lincoln said virtually the same thing in 1861 about his country. Indeed, the most fitting way to conclude this comparative analysis of ethnic and civic nationalism in the United States and Canada is with another pair of quotations 130 years apart in time, and perhaps also far apart in the stature of the speakers, but identical in purport. "We must settle this question now," said Lincoln in 1861, "whether in a free government the minority have the right to break up the government whenever they choose. If we fail it will go far to prove the incapability of the people to govern themselves." In 1991 Prime Minister Brian Mulroney warned that "the very existence of our country is at stake.... And the truth is that the end of Canada would be one of mankind's greatest failures."[6] It remains to be seen whether in Canada, as in the United States, water will prove to be thicker than blood.

NOTES

I: A Tale of Two Nations

1. Max Farrand, ed., *Records of the Federal Convention of 1787*, vol. 2 (New Haven, 1911), 449.

2. Charleston *Mercury*, February 1, 1858; New York *Tribune*, April 12, 1855.

3. The Earl of Durham and William Johnson both quoted in Ron Graham, *The French Quarter* (Toronto, 1992), 144, 214–15.

4. Most of the data in this paragraph come from the published tables of the United States Census and from *Historical*

Statistics of the United States: Colonial Times to 1957 (Washington, D.C., 1960). See also Stanley Lebergott, "Labor Force and Employment, 1800–1960," in *Output, Employment, and Productivity in the United States after 1800: Studies in Income and Wealth*, vol. 30 (New York, 1966), 131.

5. Calculated from the tables and data in *Canada Year Book 1994* (Ottawa, 1993).

6. Quoted in William Howard Russell, *My Diary North and South*, ed. Fletcher Pratt (New York, 1954), 99, 38.

7. Rupert B. Vance, "The Geography of Distinction: The Nation and Its Regions, 1790–1927," *Social Forces* 18 (1939): 175–76; Graham, *French Quarter*, 141.

8. Hugh MacLennan, *Two Solitudes* (New York, 1945), 140, 159.

9. Quotations, respectively, from J. Mills Thornton, *Politics and Power in a Slave Society: Alabama, 1800–1860* (Baton Rouge, 1978), 255; and Robert R. Russel, *Economic Aspects of Southern Sectionalism, 1840–1861* (Urbana, Ill., 1924), 48.

10. Jane Jacobs, *The Question of Separatism: Quebec and the Struggle over Sovereignty* (New York, 1980), 50–51; Peter H. Russell, *Constitutional Odyssey: Can Canadians Be a Sovereign People?* (Toronto, 1992), 73.

11. De Bow's address to a Southern Commercial Convention in New Orleans, January 1852, quoted in Herbert Wender, *Southern Commercial Conventions, 1837–1859* (Baltimore, 1930); *De Bow's Review* 13 (1852): 571; 9 (1850): 120.

12. Editorial in Huntsville *Advocate* in August 1850, quoted in Arthur C. Cole, *The Whig Party in the South* (Washington, D.C., 1913), 208.

13. Planter quoted in John McCardell, *The Idea of a Southern Nation: Southern Nationalists and Southern Nationalism, 1830–1860* (New York, 1979), 134; Hammond's speech printed in *Congressional Globe*, 35 Congress, 1 Session (1858), 961–62.

14. Robert William Fogel and Stanley L. Engerman, *Time on the Cross: The Economics of American Negro Slavery* (Boston, 1974), 248.

15. T. John Samuel, *Quebec Separatism Is Dead: Demography Is Destiny* (Ottawa, 1994), 13, 37.

16. Quoted in William Barney, *The Road to Secession: A New Perspective on the Old South* (New York, 1972), 105–106.

17. See Russel B. Nye, *Fettered Freedom: Civil Liberties and the Slavery Controversy, 1830–1860* (East Lansing, Mich., 1949).

18. Minister of justice quoted in Mordecai Richler, *Oh Canada! Oh Quebec! Requiem for a Divided Country*

(Toronto, 1992), 24; *Speech of William L. Yancey of Alabama, Delivered in the National Democratic Convention* (Charleston, 1860).

19. Dion quoted in Richler, *O Canada*, 25; Georgian quoted in Michael P. Johnson, *Toward a Patriarchal Republic: The Secession of Georgia* (Baton Rouge, 1977), 47.

20. Daniel Latouche, "Betrayal and Indignation on the Canadian Trail: A Reply from Quebec," in Philip Resnick, *Letters to a Québécois Friend* (Montreal, 1990), 89; Dunbar Rowland, ed., *Jefferson Davis, Constitutionalist: His Letters, Papers, and Speeches,* vol. 5 (Jackson, Miss., 1923), 72, 84.

21. *Congressional Globe,* 31 Congress, 1 Session (1850), Appendix, 451–55. Calhoun outlined his proposal for a concurrent majority in his posthumously published *Disquisition on Government.*

22. Kenneth McRoberts, "Introduction," in McRoberts, ed., *Beyond Quebec: Taking Stock of Canada* (Montreal, 1995), 25; Abraham Rotstein, "A Difficult Transition: English-Canadian Populism vs Quebec Nationalism," in ibid., 374.

23. Paul E. Johnson, "Toward an American Culture," in John M. Murrin et al., *Liberty, Equality, Power: A History of the American People* (Fort Worth, Tex., 1996), 355–56.

24. Quoted in Peter Brimelow, *The Patriot Game: Canada and the Canadian Question Revisited* (Stanford, Cal., 1986), 253.

25. Russell, *Constitutional Odyssey*, 79–80.

26. Quoted in Guy Laforest, *Trudeau and the End of a Canadian Dream* (Montreal, 1995), 121.

II: Ethnic versus Civic Nationalism in the American Civil War

1. *War of the Rebellion . . . Official Records of the Union and Confederate Armies*, Ser. III, vol. 1 (Washington, D.C., 1899), 72; Raleigh *Register*, May 10, 1861.

2. J. Randolph Tucker, "The Great Issue," *Southern Literary Messenger* (hereinafter *SLM*) 34 (March 1861): 187; *De Bow's Review* (hereinafter *DBR*) 30 (February 1861): 252.

3. James D. Richardson, comp., *Compilation of the Messages and Papers of the Presidents, 1789–1897*, vol. 5 (Washington, D.C., 1897), 628–37; Michael Burlingame and John R. Turner Ettlinger, eds., *Inside Lincoln's White House: The Complete Civil War Diary of John Hay* (Carbondale, Ill., 1997), 20: diary entry of May 7, 1861.

4. Philadelphia *Public Ledger*, June 7, 1861, and Indianapolis *Daily Journal*, April 27, 1861, in

Howard C. Perkins, ed., *Northern Editorials on Secession*, vol. 2 (New York, 1952), 845–47, 814–15.

5. Paul R. Brass, *Ethnicity and Nationalism: Theory and Comparison* (Newbury Park, Cal., 1991), 69.

6. Hans Kohn, *The Idea of Nationalism: A Study of Its Origins and Background* (New York, 1944), 10; Walker Connor, *Ethnonationalism: The Quest for Understanding* (Princeton, 1994), 4.

7. Connor, *Ethnonationalism*, 43, 41.

8. Guy Laforest, *Trudeau and the End of a Canadian Dream* (Montreal, 1995), 131. See also Connor, *Ethnonationalism*; Ernest Gellner, *Nations and Nationalisms* (Oxford, 1983); and Anthony Smith, *The Ethnic Origins of Nations* (Oxford, 1986).

9. Michael Ignatieff, *Blood and Belonging: Journeys into the New Nationalism* (New York, 1993), 7.

10. "Are We a Nation?" in Charles Sumner, *Works*, vol. 16 (Boston, 1877), 10–12, 42, 45–46.

11. Quoted in Liah Greenfeld, *Nationalism: Five Roads to Modernity* (Cambridge, Mass., 1992), 435.

12. Alexis de Tocqueville, *Democracy in America*, trans. by George Lawrence, ed. J.P. Mayer (New York, 1966), 378.

13. Quoted in Hans Kohn, *American Nationalism: An Interpretative Essay* (New York, 1957), 148.

14. Roy P. Basler, ed., *The Collected Works of Abraham Lincoln*, vol. 2 (New Brunswick, N.J., 1953), 355.

15. Republicans quoted in Hans L. Trefousse, *The Radical Republicans: Lincoln's Vanguard for Racial Justice* (New York, 1969), 86; Richard H. Sewell, *Ballots for Freedom: Antislavery Politics in the United States, 1837–1860* (New York, 1976), 269; Michael F. Holt, *The Political Crisis of the 1850s* (New York, 1978), 171.

16. Carl Schurz, "True Americanism," Address delivered in Fanueil Hall, Boston, April 18, 1859, in Frederic Bancroft, ed., *Speeches, Correspondence and Political Papers of Carl Schurz*, vol. 1 (New York, 1913), 57; Basler, ed., *Collected Works of Lincoln*, vol. 2, 323.

17. Emerson quoted in Howard R. Floan, *The South in Northern Eyes, 1831 to 1861* (Austin, Tex., 1958), 51; New Yorker quoted in Grady McWhiney, *Cracker Culture: Celtic Ways in the Old South* (Tuscaloosa, Ala., 1988), 1.

18. Southern travellers quoted in McWhiney, *Cracker Culture*, 1; Charles C. Jones, Jr., to Charles C. Jones, January 28, 1861, in Robert Manson Myers, ed., *The Children of Pride: A True Story of Georgia and the Civil War* (New Haven, 1972), 648.

19. Tocqueville, *Democracy in America*, 374–75.

20. Scot quoted in McWhiney, *Cracker Culture*, 1;

Englishman quoted in Rollin G. Osterweis, *Romanticism and Nationalism in the Old South* (New Haven, 1949), 141.

21. *Congressional Globe*, 36 Congress, 2 Session (1860–61), 12.

22. Russell, *My Diary North and South*, 38; Simms quoted in John McCardell, *The Idea of a Southern Nation: Southern Nationalists and Southern Nationalism, 1830–1860* (New York, 1979), 170–71.

23. Tocqueville, *Democracy in America*, 348.

24. George E. Baker, ed., *The Works of William H. Seward*, vol. 4 (New York, 1861), 289–92; Basler, ed., *Collected Works of Lincoln*, vol. 2, 461.

25. Augusta *Daily Constitutionalist*, March 30, 1861.

26. Ignatieff, *Blood and Belonging*, 85–89; Eric J. Hobsbawm, *Nations and Nationalism since 1870* (Cambridge, 1990), 12; John Hutchinson and Anthony D. Smith, eds., *Nationalism* (New York, 1994), 5.

27. *SLM* 30 (June 1860): 404–05, 407.

28. *DBR* 30 (February 1861): 162.

29. Ibid. 30 (January 1861): 45–51.

30. Louis-Philippe quoted in William R. Taylor, *Cavalier and Yankee: The Old South and the American National Character* (New York, 1961), vii; Michigan visitor quoted in Osterweis, *Romanticism and*

Nationalism, 205; Louisville editor quoted in ibid., 101.

31. Richmond *Daily Dispatch*, February 7, March 23, 1863; Henry Timrod, "Ethnogenesis," in William Gilmore Simms, ed., *War Poetry of the South* (New York, 1867), 7–11.

32. Richmond *Daily Dispatch*, September 11, 1861; September 14, 1863.

33. *SLM* 30 (June 1860): 103, 409; 31 (November 1860): 349; 33 (July 1861): 19 (August 1861), 106; *DBR* 31 (October/November 1861): 393.

34. For a discussion of the historiography of the Cavalier thesis, see David Hackett Fischer, *Albion's Seed: Four British Folkways in America* (New York, 1989), 225–26, 787.

35. Eric J. Hobsbawm and Terence Rangers, eds., *The Invention of Tradition* (New York, 1983); Benedict Anderson, *Imagined Communities: Reflections on the Origin and Spread of Nationalism* (London, 1983).

36. Osterweis, *Romanticism and Nationalism*, 136; Walker Connor, "A Nation is a Nation, is a State, is an Ethnic Group, is a . . . " in Hutchinson and Smith, eds., *Nationalism*, 37; Renan quoted in Hobsbawm, *Nations and Nationalism*, 12.

37. [Montpelier] *Vermont Watchman and State Journal*,

April 26, 1861, in Perkins, ed., *Northern Editorials on Secession*, 751–53.

38. Basler, ed., *Collected Works of Lincoln*, vol. 4 (New Brunswick, N.J., 1953), 240–41, 271.

39. Dunbar Rowland, ed., *Jefferson Davis, Constitutionalist: His Letters, Papers, and Speeches*, vol. 5 (Jackson, Miss., 1923), 202; John W. Overall, "Seventy-Six and Sixty-One," in William Shepperson, ed., *War Songs of the South* (Richmond, 1862), 62–63.

40. *SLM* 33 (July 1861): 21, 27; *DBR* 31 (July 1861): 72, 73, 76; 32 (January/February 1862): 9, 19.

41. *SLM* 37 (November/December 1863): 667, 674.

42. Richard B. Harwell, *Songs of the Confederacy* (New York, 1951), 26. This verse was part of a poem by Catherine Anne Warfield, of Kentucky, which first appeared in the *SLM* 34 (November/December 1862): 633, under the title "You Can Never Win Them Back."

43. Richmond *Daily Dispatch*, October 4, December 12, 1862; *SLM* 37 (November/December 1863): 686.

44. New Orleans *Bee*, May 1, 1861, in Dwight Lowell Dumond, ed., *Southern Editorials on Secession* (New York, 1931), 513; *DBR* 30 (May/June 1861): 681.

45. In Simms, ed., *War Poetry*, 116.

46. In Shepperson, ed., *War Songs*, 30, 41, 59.

47. Rev. E.P. Birch, "Yankee Doodle's Ride to Richmond," in ibid., 114.

48. "Captain Maffit's Ballad of the Sea," in Simms, ed., *War Poetry*, 233.

49. Edwin H. Fay to Sarah Fay, September 19, June 27, 1863, in Bell Irvin Wiley, ed., *"This Infernal War": The Confederate Letters of Sgt. Edwin H. Fay* (Austin, Tex., 1958), 329, 286–87.

50. Theodorick W. Montfort to Louisa Montfort, March 18, 1862, in Spencer Bidwell King, Jr., ed., "Rebel Lawyer: The Letters of Lt. Theodorick W. Montfort, 1861–1862," *Georgia Historical Quarterly* 49 (1965): 209; Elijah Petty to wife, September 11, 1862, in Norman D. Brown, ed., *Journey to Pleasant Hill: The Civil War Letters of Captain Elijah P. Petty* (San Antonio, Tex., 1982), 78–79.

51. *DBR* 33 (May/August 1862): 51; "The Fire of Freedom," in Simms, ed., *War Poetry*, 54.

52. *SLM* 32 (June 1861): 420–21.

53. Richmond *Enquirer*, March 16, 1863, November 2, 1864.

54. A.D. Pratt to Charles C. Murdock, February 16, 1863, Murdock Papers, Illinois State Historical Library.

55. Isaac Jackson to Moses and Phebe Jackson, July 13, 1863, in *"Some of the Boys...": The Civil War*

Letters of Isaac Jackson, 1862–1865 (Carbondale, Ill., 1960), 111–12; George M. Wise to John Wise, March 13, 1865, in Wilfred W. Black, ed., "Civil War Letters of George M. Wise," *Ohio Historical Quarterly* 46 (1957): 193.

56. Thomas T. Taylor to Antoinette Taylor, May 23, June 18, 1861, Taylor Papers, Ohio Historical Society; Titus Crenshaw to father, November 10, 1861, March 28, 1862, in Charlotte Erickson, *Invisible Immigrants: The Adaptation of English and Scottish Immigrants in Nineteenth-Century America* (Coral Gables, Fla., 1972), 348, 351.

57. Basler, ed., *Collected Works of Lincoln*, vol. 4, 438, 426.

58. London *Daily News*, September 27, 1864, quoted in Allan Nevins, *The War for the Union*, Vol. 4: *The Organized War to Victory, 1864–1865* (New York, 1971), 141.

59. Alfred L. Hough to Mary Hough, October 28, 1863, March 13, 1864, in Robert G. Athearn, ed., *Soldier in the West: The Civil War Letters of Alfred Lacey Hough* (Philadelphia, 1957), 165, 178.

60. Josiah Chaney to Melissa Chaney, October 3, 1862, Chaney Papers, Minnesota Historical Society; Robert McAllister to Ellen McAllister, April 9, 1865, in James I. Robertson, Jr., ed., *The Civil War Letters of*

General Robert McAllister (New Brunswick, N.J., 1965), 608.

61. Basler, ed., *Collected Works of Lincoln*, vol. 5 (New Brunswick, N.J., 1953), 537.

62. Howard K. Beale, ed., *Diary of Gideon Welles*, vol. 2 (New York, 1960), 276–77: entry of April 7, 1865; James Russell Lowell, "Ode Recited at the Harvard Commemoration, July 21, 1865," *Atlantic Monthly* 16 (September 1865), 369.

63. Francis Lieber, "The Latin Race," letter published in the New York *Evening Post*, 1871, in Lieber, *Contributions to Political Science* (Philadelphia, 1881), 108–109.

64. William K. Scarborough, ed., *The Diary of Edmund Ruffin*, vol. 3 (Baton Rouge, 1989), 946: entry of June 18, 1865.

Epilogue

1. William Faulkner, *Intruder in the Dust* (New York: Signet, New American Library ed., 1948), 148–49.

2. Ramsay Cook, *The Maple Leaf Forever* (Toronto, 1971), 100.

3. Michael Walzer, "Comment," in Charles Taylor, *Multiculturalism and the Politics of Recognition* (Princeton, 1992), 101.

4. John Russell Bartless, ed., *The Soldiers' National Cemetery at Gettysburg* (Providence, R.I., 1874), 100–101.

5. Quoted in Lansing Lamont, *Breakup: The Coming End of Canada and the Stakes for America* (New York, 1994), 15.

6. For source of Lincoln quotation, see Chap. II, note 3; Mulroney quoted in Lamont, *Breakup*, 15.